T0067258

When

Heat

Meets

Romance

&

The Glue factor

The Right Key Always Opens The Door

Peter B. Eta

Order this book online at www.trafford.com
or email orders@trafford.com

Most Trafford titles are also available at major online book retailers.

© Copyright 2014 Peter B. ETA.
All rights reserved. No part of this publication may be reproduced, stored in a retrieval system, or transmitted, in any form or by
any means, electronic, mechanical, photocopying, recording, or otherwise, without the written prior permission of the author.

Printed in the United States of America.

ISBN: 978-1-4907-4228-1 (sc)
ISBN: 978-1-4907-4227-4 (e)

Because of the dynamic nature of the Internet, any web addresses or links contained in this book may have changed
since publication and may no longer be valid. The views expressed in this work are solely those of the author and do
not necessarily reflect the views of the publisher, and the publisher hereby disclaims any responsibility for them.

Any people depicted in stock imagery provided by Thinkstock are models,
and such images are being used for illustrative purposes only.
Certain stock imagery © Thinkstock.

Trafford rev. 07/28/2014

 www.trafford.com
North America & international
toll-free: 1 888 232 4444 (USA & Canada)
fax: 812 355 4082

To all those who are going through relationship problems and those who are committed in making *love* a genuine gift.

ACKNOWLEDGEMENTS

With special thanks:

- to my glorious wife, Emilia, for enabling me to experience true love always

- to my loving daughter, Sarah, for just being my baby

- to my parents, Joseph and Grace, for modelling parenthood to me even through stormy situations

- to my siblings for supporting me over the years in various ways

- to my family at St Andrew's Presbyterian Church for being there for me

- above all, to my best friend, the Holy Spirit, for journeying with me in the physical and spiritual realms in life.

CONTENTS

The key

C hocolate, check! Smooth red heart shape, check! Well-nourished red roses, check! Sweet fragrance, check! Soft gentle wind, check! Soothing music, check! A seductive touch, check! Indeed a complete, irresistible package! These are highly attractive yet controversial realities that bind *love*. Also, they often stamp a sensational feeling in one's mind, especially around that special person. No wonder activities that generate sensational feelings are sometimes prescribed to those experiencing some sort of emotional imbalance. Pause for a moment and envisage having an evergreen *love* life in which its flame burns forever—a place of rest, acceptance, integrity, excitement, rejuvenation, and completion. Those who have ever been there can attest that it's truly an ideal place to be. And as one of them, I am pleased to inform you that this is the place where 'heat meets romance and the glue factor'.

With *When Heat Meets Romance and the Glue Factor* in your *love* relationship, fantasies become daily realities, and instead of oxygen, *love* keeps you alive. That is why this complete masterpiece seeks to empower you to have and/ or enjoy the best of *love* relationships irrespective of your experience, age, gender, physical appearance, prominence, or degree of commitment (single, engaged, or married). With this fuel at your disposal, you will be able to continually keep the flame burning in your *love* relationship, regardless of the controversies life throws into the flame.

But despite the blues in the controversial theme of *love*, the benefits cannot be ignored. Therefore, join me in exploring ways to give true meaning and direction to every *love* relationship, taking a *love* relationship to the next level, revitalizing an old *love* relationship, developing the must-have glue factor in you, and much more. I hope, after reading through this piece, you will be inspired to make your *love* relationship that place where heat eternally meets romance and the glue factor!

The key

Be that goldfish that brightens the fish tank

*Everybody is a goldfish, but the degree of gold seen in
you depends on the extent to which it is polished.*

We all have an outfit, meal, hairstyle, career, brand of music, city, or car that we hold in high regard. Why? Because there is something special about this item! Imagine that this is how someone you truly have feelings for thinks of you above everyone. In other words, this person sees you as that goldfish that brightens the dark world of infidelity, betrayal, loneliness, dissatisfaction, heartlessness, mediocrity, and shame.

This was what I realized a long time ago when I visited a friend for dinner who had a very big fish tank in his dining room. Before dinner was served, the lights in this room were off. And when I walked into his dining room as he showed me around his house, the first thing I noticed was the big, bright, and beautiful goldfish in this tank. For a short while, it caught my full attention, especially because though the room was dark, this fish was still very bright. Then I realized that the presence of a goldfish in a fish tank truly makes a great difference even if this tank is in a dark room.

This is the same with people and *love* relationships. The presence of the 'right' person in your life makes a great difference, even when your life is full of challenges.

Therefore, if you are already in a relationship with someone, let me ask you these questions: When everyone looks at your partner, what do they see? And when they listen to your partner, what do they hear? Is it obvious to them that, thanks to you, your partner has a beautified life? Or does all the evidence prove otherwise?

The truth is, attracting and starting a relationship with someone are not enough; you need special qualities to nourish and sustain this relationship. And one of the ways of doing this is to upgrade your ability to refine the gold in your partner. Do you want to bring out true tenderness, respect, understanding, appreciation, and much more from your partner? If yes, then you must polish up that gold in you. Why? The way you will be treated by your partner depends on the way your partner sees or thinks of you!

May I remind you that gold is very rare, expensive, and special! Therefore, only the privileged are in possession of it, and they treat it with a lot of affection. And the question everyone in a relationship consciously or unconsciously ask themselves is, Is my partner worth the extreme affection, heartfelt sacrifice, unquestionable faithfulness, and much more? Their answers are often based on how polished your gold qualities are.

And the sad truth is, if you are not that goldfish in the heart of your partner, someone else might be sooner or later. So who is it going to be, you or a passerby? Who will reap the fruits of your labour? Remember what happened to me when I saw that goldfish; it stole my full attention for a while. Therefore, what happens when your partner recognizes someone else as the goldfish *you* ought to be? The fact is, this person will receive tenderness, respect, sincerity, appreciation, provision, and much more from your partner. Why? Obviously because this is how a goldfish is treated; a special fish needs and always gets special attention. Guess what you will receive as a result? Most or all your partner's weaknesses sooner or later! Therefore, if you want to always receive special treats from your partner, you have to be that goldfish which always illuminates. But how?

You must realize and accept that—irrespective of your background, age, status, physical appearance, past or current *love* experience—you have the qualities of a goldfish. But the degree of gold seen in you depends on how polished your goldfish qualities are. In other words, the more polished these qualities are, the brighter you will be seen, and vice versa. Therefore, to achieve this objective, you must be able to ask/answer questions like these: What kind of polish will brighten me up? Do I have the brush that will enhance this polish? How long will my brightness last?

In this regard, I recommend you should mind your lifestyle, looks, friends, resources, personal grooming, relationship objective, and much more. Why? Because these factors can refine or obscure the gold in you. How? Let's take relationship objective as an example. If you get into a relationship with intentions of building an unbreakable bond and you stick to this cause no matter what happens, your unique gold qualities will be brightened as a result. But if your intention is just to have fun, sooner or later, this will cloud your gold qualities, and you will never build or have a true and lasting *love* relationship.

Interestingly, one of the reasons some people are not bright enough even though they have good intentions is that they are full of excuses, consciously or unconsciously: 'Well, I want to make him happier, but he comes home from work late at night' or 'I'd like to express more appreciation, but I don't have enough resources, such as time, money, and ideas'. Though your excuse for not being a better *lover* may be understandable, do not let excuses stand in your way to attaining real and sustainable happiness. Instead, rise up above any excuse and let your true (gold) nature shine. Don't let anyone or anything keep you down even if it might have done so for a while. It is never too late to bounce back and shine again. As long as you are alive, you have the chance to show the world how bright you can be.

Do you mean to tell me that this is the brightest you can be? Is this truly all that is in you? Has the ocean of *love* felt your most intense passion for your partner? Imagine what will happen when you tap from within and bring to the surface that which the winds of *love* have never transported into your partner's spirit. Oh! I can hear the voice of your partner calling from afar, 'My strength, hope, and sincere affection blossom proportionally to the brightness of your gold qualities.' Therefore, without further ado, I cheer you on to ignore the challenges that your *love* life may face and to be that goldfish that brightens and sustains your partner's life.

The key

You have only one chance to impress

*Don't ask for many chances to impress me
because you may not get them.*

Have you ever heard of the saying 'First impression stands out'? Well, I have another saying I'm excited to share with you: 'Don't ask for many chances to impress me because you may not get them.' And if you can impress me only when I spend more time with you, how impressive will you be when something unavoidable suddenly occupies much of my time? How often do I receive red roses, a heartfelt romantic moment, and sweet fidgeting excitement from you? It's high time you revisit my needs and treat me as though I have given you only one chance to impress me, a chance of a lifetime. And no one else has this chance but you. So what are you going to do with it?

Please, instead of telling me what you would do when you have more time in your hands, why not show me what you can do with the limited time you have? Tell me what you would do when you have more resources instead of showing me what you can do with the inadequate resources you currently have. This is exactly how anyone who has sincere feelings for you thinks. In case you've never listened to the voice of a craving lover, this is how it sounds. And sadly, many have found themselves in frail relationships because they didn't listen to the cry of their partner.

But the question I really want us to evaluate is, do moments of strong affection come and go, or can they exist always? Well, some people argue that such moments can't exist always due to tragic incidences that could destabilize your mood from time to time, causing you to react differently towards your partner. Though this sounds great, I'd like you to tell me why people go through a lot just to attract that sunshine into their lives but, when this mission is accomplished, they don't reach out to that sunshine as they used to when they were just falling in *love*. And I'd also like to know where tragic incidences were when they were just falling in *love*. Or do they exist only after the heart and soul have been given? Why blame it now on work, time, resources, and other excuses when they stopped every excuse from taking its toll when they were just falling in *love*? Why do sweet people change after being in a relationship for a while? Is it because they now know how much their partner cares for them?

Sadly, this chorus is sung by many across the world because they or their partner doesn't treat every chance as though it was the first-impression moment. As a result, familiarity and other love-breakers (which will be dealt with as you read further) take their toll. But if you find yourself in such a place, is all hope lost? The answer is no, especially when you can be the potter of your relationship, as the next chapter says! So then how can you treat each opportunity as though it is the first-impression moment?

First-impression moments are often memorable and sweet because people go an extra mile to please their prospective lover. They wear very attractive outfit, express a lot of tenderness, listen attentively, tell funny stories, and in general, they appear to be very sweet, reliable, and special. This reminded me of my first date with my wife. Before the occasion, I booked a table at a restaurant, had a special waitress for the occasion, and I waited for her at the entrance. When she arrived, I walked her to our table and pulled the chair for her to sit on, and the rest of this evening was very memorable.

But what happened several months after we started dating? Honestly, I didn't always book a table, organize a special waiter or be a great company unlike when we were just falling in *love*. Why? As time went by, I let familiarity and other excuses take their toll on me. Imagine how many relationships suffer just because each moment wasn't treated with great affection like the first-impression moment. No wonder the relationships under the toll of love-breakers become weak and boring, lose their vision, and in many cases, break up.

Therefore, to ensure that the first-impression feelings do not fade with time, you should transfer these feelings into each day of your relationship. Remember that if you are the goldfish that brightens your partner's fish tank, you'll have to be consistent in all that you do. Create a positive vibe around you. Be a great company irrespective of what time brings. Develop romantic opportunities at any time and make the most of those that just pop up. I guarantee you that there will always be incidences that will attempt to weaken your relationship, but you have to fight. And one of the ways of doing this or making sure that your relationship can easily move to the next level is to treat each moment as though it were the first-impression moment.

Honestly speaking, those who have developed the ability to treat each moment as the first-impression moment have been able to impose a renewing feeling in their partner. By this, I mean treating each moment as though it were the first-impression moment is like watering a garden repeatedly so that it doesn't get dry. And such people have been able to make their partner feel like they keep falling in *love*. They

The key

have been able to drive memorable waves of appreciation, warmth, heartfelt sensation, and *heat* into their partner's spirit. As a result, they have truly become the potter of their relationship and hence can take this relationship to any direction or level and at their convenience.

Food for thought: can you honestly at this point in time say you have the power to take your relationship to any level at your convenience?

You are the potter, and your relationship is the clay

*The strength, quality, duration, success, and direction
of your relationship are in your hands.*

I remember visiting an old gentleman as a kid. On arrival, I said to him, 'Sir, I thought this was where you live.'

'Of course, this is where I live,' he answered.

'But why do you have clay pots everywhere?' I asked.

'These pots remind me of the extent to which we as human beings could create, modify, or sustain anything we want to with our hands,' he explained.

'Whoa! This is perfectly beautiful,' I said while looking at one of the most-defined clay pots I've ever seen.

'Yeah, boy! This is one of those pots which you make thanks to a special vision in mind,' he said.

But I was not satisfied with this statement because, as a child, I used clay to make similar structures but none lasted or looked as beautiful as any of his pots even though my vision was to create perfection. So I asked him, 'How do you know that when you mix, mould, melt, brush, smoothen, and decorate the soft, wet clay, it will become as hard and beautiful as this?'

'Well, why don't I answer this question by helping you make a pot as beautiful as those in my best collection?' he said while showing me the way to his craft room with a smile.

When we got into this room, I was excited because not only was he standing by me as a 'coach' but also because this was going to be the first time I'd use my hands to build something real, sustaining, and beautiful as his.

Immediately, his phone rang.

'Hiiiiiiii, John! Thank you for calling back . . . Not a problem, I'm about to work on your requested design, which will be ready soon . . . Okay! Let me get to work . . . Bye.' Then he dropped the phone and said to me, 'That was the parliamentarian, and he wants an exceptional pot made as a special gift to his wife as part of their anniversary presents.'

'Okay! But why don't you give him one of those pots?' I said while pointing at a shelf that had his best collection.

'No, I can't do that because you are going to give him what he wants,' he said.

'But I am not a potter,' I hastily argued in defence.

'Everybody is a potter, though some are better than others due to various reasons,' he said. After convincing me for about five minutes, it was time to prove whether what he said about everybody being a potter was true or not.

I then walked to the potter's seat while he served me with basic resources required to begin with. He then guided me on what to do every step of the way as I built the requested pot. When it was ready to be transported to the furnace, I eagerly reached for it with my bare hands, but he shouted, 'No! Don't touch the pot.'

In confusion, I responded, 'But I've been touching the pot all along. Why is now an exception?'

Then he said, 'From this stage, the pot is not supposed to be touched like you wanted to, else it will be ruined because it is not yet hardened.' He then transported the pot using his tools into the hot furnace. And after some time, he removed the pot, and we decorated it as the politician wanted.

'Whoa! This is beautiful,' I said while looking at the pot and my hands in amazement. 'And I can even touch and hold it unlike before.' From then on, I realized that, with our hands, we can truly build great, beautiful, sustaining, and thriving things in life, and these of course include an exciting *love* relationship.

Sadly, a lot of relationships don't last long partly because the lovers aren't conscious of the fact that they are the potters, their relationship is the clay, and the world is the craft room. As a result, they don't know when to touch the clay and when not to. They don't know when their relationship needs more water and when it doesn't. The truth is, the beauty of a clay pot depends on the patience of a potter and the vision in his mind. No wonder people look at some relationships and envy those in them without realizing that such relationships have gone through a furnace to become as fantastic as they now look and their potters were always at work despite the challenges that potters often face.

That is why I now challenge you with these questions: With these hands of yours, what kind of a relationship have you built? Is it one that withstands the test of time or one that barely brings out the best in you? But in case you have truly built one already, I further dare you to tell me if this is all that these precious hands of yours can actually build. Is this the best kind of relationship your partner deserves? Please revisit the hidden and invigorating potentials of your hands and put them to work. Rebuild a sweeter, more sustainable, and more exciting relationship.

I remember asking the above questions to a friend of mine when she fell in *love* with a rigid guy. In fact, the best and most convenient decision at the time was to break up with this guy because he never showed much interest and efforts in the growth of their relationship. Not only did he ignore her birthdays and Valentine's Days, but also he rarely expressed his affection for her even when she did something romantic. Interestingly, he preferred to spend pleasurable time with his rough boys than with her even though he appeared to be a gentleman. Honestly, he was a weird breed.

But after I made her reflect deeply on the questions in the previous paragraph and much more, her hands became transformation tools on a mission.

'Can my hands successfully transform this guy into a better *lover*? What if I don't succeed on this mission? More especially, what if I'm hurt terribly in the course of this process?' She kept on asking these and many more questions.

Well, I said to her, 'If you don't get on this mission at the soonest possible time, someone else will. Moreover, when you want to transform anyone, you have to understand that nobody wants to change. In fact, most people become even more rigid when they realize that you want to change them. Therefore, for you to successfully transform this guy and your relationship, you must transform his mindset.

'It will be a waste of time to ask him to spend more time with you if his mind is not transformed in this regard. You will hit a dead end if you want him to change his friends and habits, and much more if his mind is not controlled by you. Instead of wasting time doing things that will win his appreciation,

14

rather spend time doing things that will enable you to control his mind. Once you are in control of his mind, you will automatically control his being and affection towards you.'

'But how do I control his mind?' she asked.

So I continued with a smile, 'Every man wants to be better financially, sexually, influentially, and in every other endeavour. But the steps most men take to achieve these goals are inappropriate, slow, haphazard, strenuous, worthless, or simply not the best. But being men, they still have to stay on their feet to make things happen. And this is where you—a beautiful, smart, sweet, and seductive lady— come in.' I said this while holding her hands in-between mine.

'If you will program your man to see better steps that he can take and effortlessly achieve greater results in all his endeavours, you will become the bearer and controller of his mind. For example, instead of asking him to spend more time with you when his busy schedule won't allow, why not ask him to give you a chance to refresh him? A refreshed man is a better achiever. Listen to the voice of a truth.

'About 90 per cent of a man's schedule is generally serious and tight because of his priorities. Therefore, besides a holiday, a man will scarcely include activities like shopping, manicuring, long pleasurable chats with anyone during the day, and much more in his schedule. So it's your responsibility to be his *major* source of excitement, peace, joy, laughter, rest, and much more. Consequently, if you know how to penetrate this tight schedule and relieve him of any pressure of the day/week, you will certainly control his mind.'

What happened next? Ha ha! She boosted him after only a short while. Instead of spending hours in the evening

15

nagging, she decided to make him enjoy a beautiful evening, which overpowered the effect of any failures he might have encountered during the day. Instead of taking lunch to him, she made him realize that during his lunch break, her arms were the place lunch tasted better. Instead of blaming him for everything, she blessed him for anything. She made time and researched more about his business ventures, and with a lot of patience, wisdom, and positive energy, she was able to be the reason he obtained better results unlike before. She never worried when he closed work late but kept her arms wide open for him to run into.

As a result, she became his favourite company which he couldn't do without, a place of no suspicion and with full acceptance, deep affection, and rejuvenating laughter. Instead of saying to him, 'I don't want you to hang out with the boys,' she said to him, 'Baby, your boys need you around to cause them to man up, so go show them what you got.' As a result, he became fond of her. By this time, he saw her as a complete package which every man out there would die for, so he started treating her like a goddess. And before she knew it, this once-upon-a-time busy and rigid business mogul was transformed into a loving and open man who classified her as his top business commitment. Today, he praises her for all his successes, joy, good health, and thriving life. Why? She understood that every man values peace, joy, laughter, excitement, and rest and can only enjoy these from a lady like her.

The point is, many relationships out there get sour or broken because of a partner who appears to be rigid in some ways. As a result, your affection towards such a person over time might be weakened, especially when you don't feel a strong and consistent vibe from your relationship. Not long after, you'll easily forget that your partner and relationship are simply that clay which probably needs just a bit of water from you in order to be fine. Once this slips off your mind, you will start to see only your partner's mistakes, which will cause you to be very critical/poisonous.

And this is definitely not the attitude of a true potter. In other words, a true potter doesn't stop being a potter simply because the clay took long to be moulded or the heat from the furnace was too hot. If only you would remind yourself in front of a challenge that you are responsible for how your relationship turns out, it will boost you to achieve the unthinkable.

Remember, *love*-breakers will always attack your relationship. But if you are not prepared to treat your partner and relationship as precious as clay is to a potter, then you will always find yourself jumping from one relationship to another, complaining about how unfortunate you are in relationships. Also remind yourself that not all clays are as smooth as the other, but in the hands of a true potter, a beautiful clay pot could still be formed from the worst clay ever. Perhaps your partner is not as smooth as you would have wanted, but now that he or she is in your hands, I believe you can make beauty where no one thought possible.

I just remembered what Michelangelo, a famous sculptor, said, 'I saw the angel in the marble and carved until I set it free.' Interestingly, this angel that he carved out from the marble became one of the greatest structures ever carved from a stone in history. But how did it come about? When Michelangelo looked at that marble, he saw an angel. When he touched the marble, he felt this angel being released, so he kept carving until this structure became a piece of formidable beauty. Just imagine that you are Michelangelo and that your partner/relationship is that angel in the marble who can only be released if you keep carving. Do you know how amazed people who knew your partner/relationship back then will be when they look this time around and instead see an angel they never thought could have been in the marble?

Dear friend! Please let's reason together. Do you agree with me on the fact that when you keep expecting your partner to be 100 per cent sweet towards you at all times, you are acting as the clay instead of the potter? Would I be speaking your mind if I say, unlike the potter, clay never shapes clay? In other words, you won't add much value to your relationship if you, just like your partner, are 'clays'. If you agree to these, then you are truly ready to take your relationship to the next level.

The key

How to take a relationship to the next level

If you want to gather honey, don't scatter the beehive.

Every relationship has levels, and it is expected that each relationship should move to the next level after some time. In other words, if it moves to the next level, it means it is growing because only growth will cause a relationship to move to the next level. This reminds me of a relationship that has lasted for about fifteen years, yet it is as though it has hit an impermeable wall; she desperately needed a ring, but he said he needed more time to think about it. And back then, they were seen as the perfect combination. In fact, they used to be the envy of other couples in those days—unlike today. Interestingly, she used to give counsel to other relationships, but she is being counselled now on how she can get a ring from him. Poor girl!

But taking a relationship to the next level is not only for singles and those in courtship; marriage also has levels, and it's expected to attain these levels except when the marriage isn't growing. And just for the record, the next level is often a better place, a meeting point of deeper intimacy, unquestionable respect, syrupy heat, continual provision, bounteous sacrifice, and genuine, reciprocated appreciation on a solid foundation of maturity and integrity. But who is supposed to do what, when, and how to ensure that this elevation is achieved? In simple terms, irrespective of the degree of roughness in your relationship, how can you take it to the next level that it ought to attain?

Understand, identify, and make use of temperaments

Be a master of the inborn nature that controls people's choices and behavioural patterns in relationships.

One of the first principles to consider before you can take any relationship to the next level is to be able to understand why people naturally behave the way they do as well as how to influence them in a particular way. I have, in a nutshell, term for this: temperament management. But what is *temperament?* This refers to a person's inborn nature, which becomes very visible as he or she grows older, and it greatly affects the person's behaviour, emotion, attention to details, relationship with people, way of reacting to situations, and much more. So at maturity, this inborn nature manifests itself in the person's behaviour each time a thought or external factor stimulates them. Therefore, if you understand temperaments fully, you will be able to effortlessly slide your relationship to the next level.

But is this applicable to every person and relationship? Well, since each and every one of us has at least a temperament, then this is very applicable to all of us. And to prove that we all have a temperament, you can go to the Internet and drop an online message that reads 'The world will end tomorrow!' Interestingly, this has happened a few times in the past. Do you want to know how people reacted? Let me tell you. Some people believed instantly, so they sold their possessions and squandered away their money. Others doubted every bit of this information, so it was business as usual for them. And some were simply nonchalant. So you see, with the same stimulus, people will naturally react differently because we all have different temperaments that largely control our reaction. Since everybody has a temperament, it means that you can influence anybody if you have full knowledge about their specific type of temperament. As a result, you will be able to eradicate about 80 per cent of your relationship problems just before they arise.

That is why I am pleased to inform you that temperament can cause your partner to endlessly fight for your relationship, and another type can cause your partner not to lift a muscle. Temperaments can also cause your partner to be very romantic, respectful, faithful, and committed to you, and vice versa. Just in case you are thinking at this point how to handle your partner's behavioural pattern/temperament, don't worry because I've got your back! Such information and much more are disclosed in the succeeding pages.

For starters, there are two major types of temperaments: introvert and extrovert.

Introverts are people who naturally keep to themselves when in a group because they are shy. Interestingly, the larger the group, the quieter they are, so you may not easily know what introverts are thinking or planning to do. As a result, they don't like outings naturally. Instead, they like to spend time in the privacy of their home so as to reflect. This explains why they are deep thinkers and slow talkers comparatively. So while in public, they generally don't smile, laugh, or express their moods. Introversion can be further divided into two groups: melancholic and phlegmatic temperaments.

Contrary to introverts, extroverts like being around people. And since they enjoy being the centre of attention wherever they are, the larger the group, the more noticeable they become. This explains why they like spending their free time in public or group gatherings. And while in a group, they do most of the talking even though they are generally poor thinkers. Also, they often go out in public with a very friendly personality, and they find it very easy to express their moods in public. Extroversion can also be divided into two categories: sanguine and choleric temperaments.

Extroverts

- Sanguine

They have a very forward or bold personality, are good talkers, and like to express their opinion in public regardless of the format. Due to the fact that it is easy for them to express their opinion, they tend to be very candid. They are also very sociable, outgoing, like working in groups, very humorous, very compassionate, and easily moved to tears. Most sanguine people also tend to be highly attracted to the opposite sex because they have a very high sensual personality and connect better to the erotic world. And when it comes to making decisions, they are to a great extent very indecisive, especially in serious matters that affect their lives. They are also very impulsive; they make decisions before thinking about the consequences.

- Choleric

This is arguably the strongest temperament. This group of individuals have self-confidence regardless of the environment or the subject of discussion they are involved in. They naturally want everyone to know and accept their point of view since they consider theirs to be better. They are very persuasive and quick to take decisions. One interesting aspect of them is that they pay attention to their presentation and physical appearance as well as that of others. Those with this temperament have proven to be born leaders, great spokesmen, and are very optimistic. In all their endeavours, their ultimate goal is to become famous or to be remembered by everyone. And this is because their pride is very important to them. As a result, the way you talk to them should be taken into consideration as they are easily offended. But I like them because they are strong-willed and very positive, so they are always determined to make a success out of any project they embark on. I think this is one of the reasons they like people, things, and assignments so as to invest their best in them.

Introverts

- Melancholic

Those with this temperament are extremely self-conscious of what they say, how to say it, where, when, and to whom. Though they often have great ideas, they are very shy in a group. As a result, they are easily embarrassed. Therefore, they prefer to work alone and pay great attention to details to ensure excellence while avoiding any chance to be humiliated. Sadly, if any mistake is done by them or by others, they will easily blame themselves. So in order to be safe, they are very slow in decision-making and are not go-getters in general. Since they are generally not comfortable talking in public, they tend to keep to themselves and hence are usually very secretive. Though they cannot initiate a conversation, they will say a thing or two when spoken to, especially while in their comfort zone or subject. Unfortunately, they are more negatively inclined with regards to their observation. This explains why they are very critical, are great analysts, and are very assumptive. Interestingly, they are very passionate about things and people, just like those with the choleric temperament.

- Phlegmatic

They are slow in all their endeavours. One questionable aspect about them is that they have and express the same mood despite changes in situations. This is partly because they are not easily moved by information. Interestingly, a phlegmatic person is only slightly excited by any impression made upon him; he has scarcely any inclination to react, and the impression vanishes quickly. They are also shy to talk freely in public, so they tend to be very reserved. A close and cross-examination of them will reveal that they are full of words/dreams but don't take actions to bring these to pass because they are full of what ifs. Therefore, they can stay on a spot for a very long time irrespective of what happens around them. They like being idle and are full of excuses and like unnecessary details when you listen to them. One of the strongest aspects about them is that it's almost impossible to convince them when their minds are made up.

In addition to the above, it is also important to note that there are some people who possess more than one temperament even though only one of these temperaments will be manifested. Such people are called those with *mixed temperaments*. For example, someone might possess both the sanguine and choleric temperaments. Such people are often difficult to deal with because you may not know which temperament will be manifested at any given time. Furthermore, there are those who have a temperament, but you can't tell of its presence because they have learnt to suppress it. Honestly speaking, those in this category are the most difficult to deal with because they won't express their thoughts for you to know what to expect from them.

Therefore, in order to successfully deal with a person's temperament, you have to make the most of their strengths while managing their weaknesses for the success of your relationship.

Sanguine

- Strengths

  - They are very communicative, chatty, and associate easily with strangers.
  - Since they are very compassionate, they always look for ways to cheer up a sad person around them.
  - Also, they are very good at reprimanding people without making the reprimanded greatly embarrassed.
  - Even though offended and they easily express their anger, they bear no resentment against you thereafter.
  - As indicated earlier, they are very candid. Therefore, they find it easy to express or admit to their weaknesses and difficulties.
  - In addition, they find it very easy to obey an authority or decision unlike those with the choleric temperament.

- Weaknesses

  - Due to the fact that a sanguine person is very compassionate, they tend to make decisions based on their feelings at the moment and pay little attention to the consequences.
  - Sadly, most people with this temperament find it very challenging to successfully build and sustain something great because they naturally don't pay detailed attention to circumstances, are not patient, easily lose interest in things, and scarcely see or foresee difficulties.
  - Since they are not deep thinkers, they are greatly influenced by the external—meaning, if you present yourself very well to a sanguine, they will be more inclined towards your looks. As a result, they can easily be flattered.
  - They love company and amusement because they always want to enjoy life. But unfortunately, in their

amusements, they easily go out of hand, especially with the opposite sex.

Choleric

- Strengths

  - Since they like being the centre of attention, they can go the extra mile to achieve the extraordinary in every aspect of their lives.
  - They are strong-willed and almost difficult to be shaken off their vision. Therefore, in the face of any obstacle, they can make sacrifices just to ensure that they end up achieving that great vision.
  - They can rush and grab opportunities while others prefer to stay far and study the situation over time, thereby missing their chance because the choleric person grabbed it already.

- Weaknesses

  - A choleric person doesn't like to be challenged by anything or anyone. So they are constantly in unnecessary competition and will stay there until they win. Sadly, they don't mind doing whatever it takes to win and be respected by all.
  - Therefore, they find it very easy to insist that you must do things a particular way, irrespective of your inabilities or the negative consequences that their decision has on either of you. Sadly, their ego can cause them to blame you when things go wrong instead of taking the blame.
  - Also, when they make decisions, they don't consider dreadful consequences, but they deeply consider how much they will be cheered by people. Therefore, a choleric person who doesn't know how to swim can

easily run into a pool to save a drowning person because he wants to be seen as a hero.

- And due to the fact that their ego is very important to them, not only do they tend to think so highly of themselves, but they can easily hurt you when you threaten their ego in any way. Sadly, a choleric person doesn't mind hurting you in public, just like they don't mind hurting the entire world for the same reason.

Melancholic

- Strengths

  - They naturally enjoy spending a lot of time self-reflecting. As a result, they often give good counsels to people.
  - They are good-hearted, dependable, and very cautious. These make them very keen to help mankind and express great sympathy towards all.

- Weaknesses

  - As deep thinkers, when they make any mistake in life, they can spend a lot of time alone just hurting as they rethink this mistake endlessly.
  - As a result, they become a burden or disinterested company to those around them in one way or another.
  - Furthermore, when a melancholic person is hurt repeatedly, irrespective of the offence, they may never forgive you or forget about it.
  - Sadly, they are very suspicious of people and happenings around them because they can easily see things from the dark side. Therefore, impressing them is to an extent difficult.
  - Due to their love for people, they find it very difficult to correct people. As a result, people often take this for weakness and make a mockery of them.

- And since they are deep thinkers, it is difficult to cause them to act quickly. Therefore, they generally and often act slowly in an emergency.

Phlegmatic

- Strengths

  - They work slowly, but perseveringly, if the work does not require much thinking.
  - They are not easily frustrated either by offenses, failures, or sufferings. Rather, they remain composed, thoughtful, deliberate, and have a cold, sober, and practical judgement.
  - Generally, they have no intense passions and do not demand much from life.

- Weaknesses

  - They are naturally inclined to an easy life: eating, drinking, watching TV, and playing because most of them arc lazy.
  - Also, they generally have no ambition and do not aspire to rule the world as a choleric person does.

But how are temperaments useful in *love* relationships? Let's take a close look at each.

Sanguine

Since they are very attracted to the opposite sex, it is your duty to monitor and separate them from social gatherings when it gets intense. Though this duty may be challenging and may sometimes result to a fight between you two, you have to still find ways to achieve this goal. Also, bear in mind that a sanguine person cannot stay at home always even if he or she loves you so much, so don't waste your resources trying to make them stay away from socializing. Therefore, the question I suggest you should answer is, How can you permit your sanguine partner to socialize cheerfully (perhaps in your absence) while causing no harm to your relationship?

This is simple. When you go out with your partner, make sure that through your gestures, those around should feel your distinctive presence. This will cause them to be conscious of the extent to which they relate with your partner. And since your partner will sometimes socialize without you, it's your responsibility to make your partner believe that those out there need his presence because they see him as a role model, but you should further make your partner know that people will appreciate him even more when he makes and spends quality time with you alone. Once your sanguine partner has this mindset, he will talk and act in public as a role model, as well as invest a lot in your private time.

Also, since they are easily moved by external factors, you are obliged to always make them see and interact with the best from you. Let your outfit be a way of expressing your affection to them, and much more, be refined and deep.

Furthermore, you should create special time to have an intimate chat with such people since they generally don't think deep and are slow decision-makers. Such chats should be done in an environment which also convenes a message similar to what you are sharing with your partner. For example, if you want to tell your sanguine partner that you are very lucky to be in love with them, use red roses and craft these words on the bed: 'I'm happy to be yours.' Remember, what they see and interact with has a greater and deeper impact on them than what you may say to them.

If your partner is sanguine, you unfortunately don't have to take their promises seriously because they rarely keep a promise unless with your help. And when you extend a helping hand, take care. Make your partner believe that you have full and sincere confidence in them; it is your place to always double-check that they have done what they have promised. And in the process, be very sweet as you tell them that nobody can fulfil these promises as good as they would and that is why you are relying on them to complete this task by the agreed time.

Also, a sanguine partner generally does not keep secrets but *must* tell someone else sooner or later. Therefore, though you shouldn't keep secrets away from your partner, it is advisable to share with them a censored/brighter side of the same information, a version which will not hurt you when you realize that they've told someone else. But after you have moulded your sanguine partner, you may open up to them with confidence.

In addition, use their comfort zone (in a group or in public) to bring out the best in them. How about using the social network to tell others how special your sanguine partner is? At times while in a public gathering, address them with a very sweet and sincere voice, with titles like *heater*, *honey*, *sweetheart*, or *babylistic baby*. Do you want to know what your partner will do as a result? Try and see . . .

Choleric

As indicated earlier, those with this temperament have a very strong regard for their ego. And as a result, they naturally lean towards those who support their ego. This therefore means that when they make a good decision but have a poor method to achieve their objective, it is better to magnify this decision, then suggest a different way through which they can achieve a greater result as well as recognition from people. In this way, their pride and interests are protected.

Since they are strong-willed, very positive, and always determined to make a success out of any project they embark on, why not make your relationship the project which will put their strength to the test? All you have to do is make them believe that, despite your efforts, the success of this relationship depends on them and that this relationship plays a great role to others out there. A choleric person is truly a great benefit to your relationship and other endeavours, especially when he knows that all eyes are on him to impress them. Such a mindset, which certainly puts a choleric person under the spotlight, causes him not to rest until all is well with your relationship. And please don't be offended by this, but they are naturally more energized under the spotlight than under your desires or demands. Therefore, I suggest you should take advantage of what they are while you build a great *love* relationship with them.

Like I said earlier, they don't mind spending the rest of their lives competing with others and will stop at nothing until they win. Therefore, you have to make them believe that their opinions, ways of doing things, and much more supersede those of others. So encourage them to keep to themselves because only fake items seek ways to convince everyone that they are the original item. Moreover, even original items look brighter when polished; therefore, they will certainly and publicly be far better than others if they learn from the strength and weaknesses of others. If you want to cause your choleric partner to suppress his limitations while maximizing his strength, this is a sure approach to go about it.

Sadly, a person who has this temperament can intentionally hurt you so badly just because you make them feel insecure or undermined. In fact, they can even kill you just in the heat of the moment, so be careful.

Just like a sanguine person, a choleric person is easily turned on in public. Since they like being in control or above everyone else, they expect you as their *lover* to always be appealing in public. This is one of the best ways to influence your choleric *lover*'s emotions for you. As long as you are able to whoa the public with your looks, prominence, mode of expression, and charisma, expect respect, appreciation, and a stronger affectionate bond from your choleric partner. Remember, they will naturally seek to be more appreciated by the public above anyone, so your contribution in this regard is unquestionable.

Melancholic

If your partner is a melancholic, why not make them believe that they are the flavour of this relationship? Remember, those with this temperament are deep thinkers, and they pay great attention in producing excellence so that they will not be blamed or seen as failures. And as said before, they often give good counsel. Therefore, should you entrust such a responsibility unto them, they will build a firm and long-lasting relationship with all that they have. Seductively and genuinely persuade your partner to accept the fact that though you want your relationship to be that place of rest, *heat*, rejuvenation, completion, and real intimacy, this can be realized only when your partner is in charge.

Since they don't like talking a lot, you have to engage them more in action than in words. How about giving them a compass as a special gift and let it do the talking for you? A melancholic partner will easily understand that you gave them this compass because you acknowledge them as the guide to that bright future.

In addition, when dealing with anyone with this temperament, if possible, minimize the number and kind of people you introduce them to because this makes them uncomfortable. Rather, try to grow your relationship around a limited group. Remember that their most comfortable zone is when they operate among a limited number of people.

Therefore, use this to your advantage to bring out the best and *love* in them.

Also, you must be very careful as you deal with a person who has this temperament because they are suicidal and may show no signs beforehand. A melancholic person can make love with you daily yet deeply angry with you because of something you did a while ago. Remember, they are very good in keeping secrets even if it means doing this for decades. Therefore, to make your melancholic partner express their deep and sincere emotions to you, always be prepared to listen and hear their heartbeat. Learn to listen between the lines, and make sure you fulfil every promise you make, else they won't remind you but will be greatly hurt. Fulfilling your promises will build great trust in them because they will be certain that if they empty themselves to you, you will take serious consideration to this effect.

Since they generally and often act slowly in an emergency, try to minimize emergences around them. Always seek ways to pre-inform them of future commitments that concern them so as to give them enough time to think and act accordingly. Also try to develop a great sense of responsibility and trust in them; this can be done by asking them to represent your relationship in certain endeavours, such as checking and informing you of all your newly received emails daily. Such an approach towards a person with this temperament wins them over easily.

In addition, use their comfort zone to bring out the best in them. How about spending much time away from public gatherings or the social network? Always seek for ways to spend quality time with your partner in private. And during such times, don't bring the public into it; for example, don't talk about your colleagues, friends, or mates because those with the melancholic temperament easily think others are better than them, especially when you talk about others always. And since they are deep thinkers, give them something memorable to think about. Let each time spent between you two speak for itself. Try to do for them what you normally don't like doing because gestures in this regard have a long-lasting effect on a melancholic.

Phlegmatic

If you are in a relationship with someone who has this temperament, you should pre-inform them of anything you want them to do since they are slow in all their endeavours. And don't stop there; further suggest easy ways through which they can achieve what you want them to. Then with a lot of patience, support, and wisdom, always monitor them to ensure they carry out the task.

Since a person with this temperament is not easily moved by information, you have to always try as much as possible to ensure they believe that your feelings for them is not only true but renewed daily. And this has to be convincing enough, else they may not believe you. To achieve this, while watching TV with them, play footsies. Always be the first to request to spend quality time with them. Never forget important things about them. Always celebrate special events, like the day you first met, kissed, made *love,* or had a milestone of some sort. Also, remember that any impression made on a phlegmatic person dies after a short time, so you have to be consistent in expressing your *love* for them.

If you keep communicating with your phlegmatic partner like this, sooner or later, you will have a great influence over his feelings. And such influence doesn't vanish easily.

And like I said earlier, they have and express the same mood despite changes in situations. Consequently, you should always prompt them to react, using questions like: What do you think? Is this better than the other? Will I make you happier if we stay at home and watch TV or when we rather go out for dinner? Their answer to such questions will give you an idea of their mood at that moment.

As revealed earlier, they can stay on a spot for a very long time, irrespective of what happens around them—meaning, even if every relationship around the world is moving to the next level, they will not be moved. This is dangerous because, unlike a choleric, a phlegmatic partner finds it comfortable leaving your relationship at a particular level forever.

Maybe you are expecting a ring or a fresh flare to your relationship, but he will not be moved even if this is very important to you. Please don't be offended by this; rather, realize that once you chose to *love* a phlegmatic person, it's your duty to lead your relationship to the next level slowly and innovatively. Remember, they are full of what ifs, so always let them see the brighter side of things. Perhaps make it clear to them the precautionary measures you have taken to ensure all goes well. And when you achieve anything, remind them of the precautionary measures you took and how they have helped you successfully. With this approach on the go, you will to an extent build a positive environment around your partner, and he won't be an obstacle as you take this relationship to the next level.

Since they have no intense passion and do not demand much from life, don't constantly disturb them with your big dreams. Also, respect their dreams even though they're often small. But you can cause a phlegmatic person to dream and achieve a very big dream if you know how. Break down what you want him to achieve into bits. Then, do not make him see the link between these dreams. Also, let him go after each, slowly but surely. In the end, when all these are put together, he will then realize that he has just achieved a great dream.

Having known the different temperaments and how each can be used to take any relationship to the next level, I suggest you should also realize that it's advisable to be in a relationship with someone of a different temperament as you. Why? Just imagine two phlegmatic people in a relationship; the relationship will be very dull and boring. And if two choleric people are in a relationship, who will submit to the other's ego? This is true because each temperament has specific needs that can be met easily and satisfactorily by someone with a different temperament. Therefore, let's look at how you can take your relationship to the next level with knowledge of your needs and of the needs of your partner.

Know and satisfy the needs of your partner

In my early teenage years, I remember that a close neighbour of ours broke up with his girlfriend when she was visiting on one occasion. I noticed this because she was crying bitterly as a result and refused to be comforted. As young as I was, I had to wonder why he left her. Seriously, she was beautiful and very friendly to everyone. And she always visited to keep him company, cook, clean, and much more. 'Who wouldn't want a special lady like her?' I questioned. 'Well, I think I know someone who wouldn't want her—this dude!'

And just when I thought the show was over, he started having an affair with another lady who was also beautiful but never cooked or cleaned for him. 'Okay! Could he have been looking for a lady who doesn't cook or clean? Maybe grown-up men prefer ladies who make them suffer,' I thought. But I even got more confused because my mom was hands-on at home, yet my dad's affection for her grew stronger. Therefore, my conclusion at this point was, there are two kinds of grown-up men—those who prefer a lady who makes them suffer and those who prefer a lady who doesn't.

But as I became active in this regard, I understood a very important principle about relationships—know the needs of your partner, and be the best person who can satisfy them. But here is the catch. A lot of people spend a while in relationships, satisfying the *wants* of their partner. Unfortunately, the question they fail to answer as a result is that if they spend their all satisfying their partner's *wants*, who is going to satisfy their partner's *needs*? Sadly, if it's not going to be you, then it will definitely be someone else. Why? Needs are those aspects that we can't do without.

For example, most men can do without a beautiful and sophisticated woman, but they can't do without a happy sex life. In other words, though they want to have an attractive woman, they need and crave for the 'erotic queen'. And sadly, unlike needs, it is easier to find someone who can satisfy your wants. Therefore, those who have gained mastery on how to identify and satisfy the needs of the opposite sex have a say in the poem of *love*. But how can you identify and satisfy the needs of your partner?

Simple! When you *look* at your partner, try to *see* beyond the external. And when you listen to your partner's voice, please hear its cravings. Also, when you *listen* to that voice talking to you, please *hear* its cravings and grant its wish. And when you are *touched*, *feel* the emotional message that your body decodes. For as long as you keep looking at your partner without seeing, listening without hearing, and touching without feeling, you will be unable to take your relationship to the next level. The fact remains that those who can see, hear, and feel the heat flux around their partner are the only ones who can satisfactorily identify and meet the needs of their partners. Consequently, they are the only ones who can successfully uplift their relationship to any level they desire. Why? Since they can handle their partner's needs at this level, their partner will consciously/unconsciously trust them to do likewise in the next level. Therefore, don't compromise.

Do not compromise

Do you know that a lot of ladies get married to men who are abusive emotionally, financially, or physically? And what surprises me is that the best reason such women could come up with is 'I thought he would change after the marriage'. Please get this straight—relationships have levels. And each level has its own challenges that *must* be dealt with as well as sacrifices that *must* be made. If you both aren't coping at this level, what makes you so certain that you would cope satisfactorily at the next level? The truth is, in most cases, the extent to which you're coping at the present level is a reflection of what you should expect at the next level.

When I had Sarah, my first child, I realized at some point in her development that she sat on her own, and as time went by, she started to crawl, stand, and walk chronologically. Just imagine what would have happened if I had forced her to start walking when she could barely sit on her own. The result would have been a fall and possibly an injury! In the same way, every level in a relationship should be considered as a place of nurturing and growth.

If these objectives are not met at this level, please don't go to the next level because this relationship is not strong enough to exist at a higher level. Should you stubbornly get into the next level, expect to interact with the nightmare side of your partner that you have never thought of before. In other words, be prepared to spend most of your time sooner or later doing damage control. Therefore, I encourage you to be careful while making a decision whether or not your relationship should go to the next level.

But what if you took this decision already, went to the next level, and found yourself in a mess? Though you should not have compromised in the first place, all hope is not lost as you can fix this. How? Firstly, don't try to take things back to the way they were. Why? Such a move is not only wrong but also proves to your partner that whenever you guys go to the next level and face challenges, you will comfortably go back to the previous level since you can't stand such challenges. With this in mind, your partner will at some point be reluctant to move your relationship to the next level even if it's the right time for this to happen.

Also, trying to take things back to the way they were indirectly exposes the amount of strength you have to operate at higher levels. Rather, the next thing you should do if you regrettably find yourself at a level you're not happy with is to tolerate, enhance, and direct. Generally, every relationship that attains a higher level puts strain on the couple to some degree. As a result, one or both partners will express an amount of frustration on the other even though they're truly in *love*. Unfortunately, at some point, those in such a situation might fight each other instead of fighting the challenges at hand.

But to win this fight against those challenges, you have to be able to tolerate your partner's frustration and his/her inability to cope at this level. And while tolerating, you should find ways to enhance your partner's strength so that together you can fight and sustain your relationship at this level. Mind you, your relationship's success at this level is not necessarily based on how much effort your partner puts in but greatly depends on your persistency and ability to enhance your partner's strength while working as a team with a vision. Above all, you should stay focused on directing your efforts and resources towards the growth and sustainability of your relationship.

But what do you do when you find yourself in a place where the only option is to compromise? Well, I know of a married couple who chose not to ever have kids because they could not cope with one. Shockingly, despite their efforts to prevent pregnancy, the woman became pregnant, and not even an abortion could terminate this pregnancy. To add to the shock was the sonar result that showed that she was going to have triplets. What were they going to do? They have just found themselves in a place where they are forced to compromise.

Interestingly, he never wanted her to have children because he doesn't want to make love after the children are born, to a mother. Also, his job was at this time very demanding. As a result, she never wanted to deal with the strain motherhood will bring to their relationship. What was going to happen after their three children were born? Was he going to cheat on her? Are there possible depression issues that this couple have to deal with sooner or later? Dear friend, things like this happen to relationships out there. But what do you do when such a thing happens to yours?

Well, when faced with a compromising situation, use the method I call AADIMO (*A* for *accept*, *A* for *adapt*, *D* for *develop*, *I* for *implement*, *M* for *monitor*, and *O* for *overcome*). You cannot adapt, develop, monitor, and overcome what you haven't accepted. Therefore, accept the situation so that you will be able to face and deal with it appropriately. Remember, accepting the situation in this context doesn't mean giving up.

Next, find ways to adapt your plans, resources, loved ones, schedule, and emotions to the situation, bearing in mind that these adjustments are only temporary. At this point, you should realize that if you don't take the next step (developing a sustainability and exit strategy) you will never overcome.

Then implement and monitor the sustainability and exit strategy you developed.

Please note that whether you are in a compromising situation or in a state where you want your relationship to move to the next level, you *must* make use of the right timing.

Make use of the right timing

Speaking of pregnancy, when a woman is pregnant, her pregnancy goes through three trimesters. And as it moves from one trimester to the next, it is advisable that she should eat, drink, and do certain things at different stages. Why? Simply because there is time for everything! What the baby needs in the first trimester is not exactly what he needs in the second and third trimesters. So if the pregnant woman wants to successfully take her pregnancy to the next trimester, she must do what is needed of her at this trimester. If in the first trimester she feeds the baby with nutrients that are not very needed now unlike in the last trimester, her baby's growth may not be the best. Also, a pregnant woman must avoid taking alcohol, smoking cigarette, and stressing herself out because these can surely deform or kill the baby.

In the same way, if you are serious about taking your relationship to the next level, you have to mind what you feed it with at this level, else it will never attain your desired level. Like I said earlier, every level that your relationship attains should be considered a nourishment and growth stage. And of course, you should be able to walk with the right time.

I remember a relationship that fell apart a week after it started because he wanted her to start cooking, cleaning, and spending nights at his house while she wanted him to change her wardrobe and car. Well, I don't think anything is wrong with what either of them wanted, but I know their timing in doing these things was wrong. In fact, when a relationship attains a certain level, requesting for a new car, sleepovers, and much more are rather considered a privilege.

Also, in every *love* relationship, there is a time (moment, day, or period) that your partner desires you more than ever. This is the time in which your partner's soul longs for yours, his heartbeat speak louder than his words, and his craving supersedes what he truly requests for. This is not the time for excuses or the time to miss at all. Therefore, be quick to sense such times and reciprocate with your soul, heartbeat, and cravings because without these, there will be no connection between you guys at this time.

The key

How to redefine an old love relationship

A tablet of pure gold doesn't cease to be gold
just because it is covered with dust.

When a *love* relationship is born, it is often a happy moment for those involved. But as they are transported by the wagon of time, a lot happens—good, bad, and ugly. These have a way of inevitably unshackling the romance and heat from a relationship over time. As a mighty wind, they possess great potential to blow out the flame of your romantic candle, then darkness and the smell of the candle's smoke become all that are left of your relationship if care is not taken as time passes by. And when this happens, your partner becomes too familiar with you and starts taking your needs for granted. And as a result, just like the waves subside as they reach the shores, so does the affection in your relationship over time.

But the good news I have for you is that as long as there is a candle, there can be a flame. As long as a relationship still exists, its passion can be reignited. In fact, it can be reborn into that place where heat meets romance and the glue factor if you know what to do.

Who said it is an old *love* relationship?

Before redefining your old relationship, it is important to answer one question: who said it is an *old love relationship,* you or your partner? Remember that if you are the one who says your relationship is an old one, the way you would go about redefining it will be different from when your partner says your relationship is old. Also, note that whosoever said that this relationship was old feels a strange aura and sees a dark cloud around your relationship.

The concern is, this person knows that strange auras often create an arena conducive for anger, bitterness, unforgiveness, distrust, unfaithfulness, and above all, a severe crack of some sort between you two sooner or later. This person further realizes that heavy rainfall usually comes after dark clouds have gathered. Therefore, a round of applause should be given to who said your relationship is an old one because it is a step towards a romantic rebirth. The next thing to do as you try to revitalize an old relationship is to identify what makes your relationship old.

Identify what makes your relationship old

Why? You can only deal with what you have identified. Your relationship is not going to be rejuvenated just because you said or agree that it's an old relationship, but it will be if you identify what makes it old and do something about it. But what really makes a relationship old?

These include simple things like, between you two, there is little or no anxiousness to spend quality time together; there is a consistent feeling of unappreciation in your relationship; either of you needs a reason before you make heartfelt sacrifices for your relationship; you guys persistently endure more than you enjoy; you don't feel intense and long-lasting passion around each other; you scarcely express your affection for your partner and vice versa; little romantic deeds are done but are not noticed; you or your partner can easily become second place in some or most endeavours; you or your partner easily gives excuses why things turned out the way they did; between you two, there is more tension and less play; and much more.

While dealing with these, I suggest you should identify and deal with the cankerworms that exist in old *love* relationships.

Identify and deal with the cankerworms that exist in old love relationships

Familiarity is one of the greatest threats that are responsible for transforming a relationship into an old one. It often causes people to lose respect and deep affection for each other after a while of being together. Therefore, when it springs forth in your relationship, realize that its only intention is to destroy the passion between you two. Familiarity can make your partner not to feel your presence when you are around as well as your absence when you are not around. Sadly, when your partner becomes too familiar with you, the sacrifices that you make may not be noticed or fully appreciated as a result. And in most cases, your partner may even find it hard to always express strong affection towards you.

But what causes familiarity? As a relationship grows, you two become closer. And the closer you become, your partner sees your weaknesses or limitations clearer and deeper unlike before. This explains why your same body that your partner fell in *love* with might after some time be seen as not good enough even though this was not your partner's view back then. Interestingly, another cause of familiarity in *love* relationships is that people slow down on personal nourishment and growth after a while in a relationship. If this is your story, be assured that your partner will become used to the same old you for a long period of time; as a result, your partner will treat you accordingly. Therefore, how can you deal with familiarity?

My prescription is *nourish* and *attract*! If you don't want your partner to become very familiar with you, then you have to spend quality and consistent me time nourishing and enhancing your *regalia*. Get back to every aspect of your life and spice it up with a better aroma. For example, grow your romantic life so that it becomes as refreshing as cold drink on a dry throat, as redefining as soft music in a troubled soul, as penetrating as an outstanding impression, as anticipated as the ray of light in a dark room, and as certain as the sun rises in the east. And after nourishing yourself, attract your partner's attention with just a 'beep'. And as your partner comes closer, with a leaping heart and surprised eyes, he or she will always desire to interact with the *nourished you*. As a result, your partner will never be familiar with you. And to achieve this, I suggest you should polish the person *in* and *on* you. How? Develop a more mature mindset and enhance your looks from time to time; in short, just be that goldfish that brightens your partner's fish tank.

Another cankerworm that easily transports a sweet relationship into an old one is *pressure.* Those who have dated for a while are pressurized to get engaged and married; those who have been married for a while are pressurized to have a child or two and, in most cases, at least a son; and those who have children or grandchildren are pressurized to devote their time and other resources nurturing these children to have a brighter future. Also, factors like health and financial status of the couple, their mates, and the society at large can induce a lot of pressure on their relationship, especially if these factors exist in the relationship for a long period of time.

And just for the record, a lot of people think the characteristic of a blossoming relationship is that there should be little or no problems between the couple and that this relationship should move faster than others. Whether this is true or false, the point is, nowadays, more admiration is given to relationships that move faster and appear to have no problems. Therefore, with this in mind, those in *love* relationships pressurize themselves to be seen as those who have it all under control.

That is why some of them make decisions based on the impression they want people to get rather than on the consequences of such decisions. As a result, most choose to hide the pressure that attack their relationship instead of dealing with it effectively. And once these are not dealt with as they should be, this relationship will become an old and tired one sooner or later.

But if you are in an old relationship, how can you deal with these pressures so as to make the relationship young and flamboyant again? Never forget or let go of why you and your partner came together in the first place—because of *love*. And any time you feel like there is an amount of pressure on your relationship just as strong as the waves of the sea, simply hold tight to this pillar/reason on which your relationship was built. If you don't, this pillar might eventually be washed away by the flood of pressure. Please remember that there will always be pressure around your *love* relationship, but there will not always be intense passion between you two, unless you wise up.

You are the charger of your partner's battery; never forget this

If you have an electrical appliance, you will agree with me that current or battery is needed to make this appliance work effectively. And as for those appliances that need a battery to operate, you have to recharge this battery always so as to avoid the appliance from switching off because of a discharged battery. What if I tell you that you are the charger of your partner's battery? What if I prove to you that you have all it takes to revitalize your partner irrespective of how dead your partner's drive towards you may be? And for your *love* relationship to be ablaze romantically and consistently, a combination of fresh water, mild sunlight, and fertile soil have to be a reality between you two. But where will these ingredients come from? Who has to flush these into the relationship? The charger of the relationship—you!

And when you study the relationship between a charger and a battery, you would know that one very reliable thing about the charger is that, irrespective of how low the battery is, the charger still has the ability to fully recharge the battery. Therefore, no matter how old your relationship is or how cold your partner's desire towards you may be, you still have what it takes to infuse excitement, sweet heat, and uplifting passion into your relationship. Also, for the charger to charge the battery effectively, it *must* be connected to the battery. Therefore, I encourage you not to be hands-off in your relationship, else its passion will quench easily. Rather, stay connected to it, for this is the only way through which you can influence it to the direction that you want.

Interestingly, there are some appliances that don't operate very well unless they have been fully charged. This is also true with some people in relationships; for them to go an extra mile for you, they have to be fully charged. For them to *love* you unconditionally and passionately, you have to first recharge them with hope, trust, faithfulness, true romance, long-lasting affection, unstoppable sacrifices, and much more. Just like chargers generally recharge batteries over time, you might have to recharge your partner too over a period of time; don't rush.

Be that playmate your partner can't find elsewhere

Just as the deer pants for the waters, so does a *love* relationship long for sensual moments. These are pleasurable moments that range from erotic chats, affectionate hugs, and hand/foot teasing to romantic kisses and sexual intercourse. Though everybody likes such moments, it is important to note that not everybody is highly stimulated by the same stimulus. In other words, some are highly stirred by erotic chats, others are stirred by sexual intercourse, and others are stirred by something else. As a result, anything less than their peak stimulus will barely scratch the surface!

So if you want to penetrate very deep into your partner's being, you have to identify what truly stirs your partner as well as to what degree. Perhaps you should also consider the fact that there is always the most conducive place/ atmosphere and time in which sensual moments have the strongest effect. For some people, the bedroom is unquestionably their favourite stadium; for others, a romantic kiss at night by the beach while fireworks brighten the sky is their most appealing moment; and there are those who can't resist intense erotic chats, especially through the Internet.

But I suggest you realize that how you play determines how long your partner will feel the impact of the sensual moment. A lot of people value the three-course-meal approach when it comes to sexual intercourse, others value deep silence or hand/foot teasing. There are those who value a bit of hair-brushing during affectionate hugs, and without a doubt, many cherish romantic music while they affectionately cuddle.

Therefore, the profound question I suggest you should answer is, from whom will your partner enjoy the most intimate sensual moments? In other words, this is a need that someone has to satisfy, and whoever is going to stir up your partner must be that *master chef* who knows how to *cook* and *serve* your partner's *favourite meal*. I am talking about someone who not only knows what spices to use but also knows how to bring them all together and at the appropriate time. Perhaps you are very good in *cooking* and *serving* a particular *meal*, but is this *meal* your partner's favourite?

The key

The glue factor

When it's all been said and done, what brings everything together?

While in a relationship with someone, you may not have complete control of whom they meet, where they go, whom they look at, their opinion about people, and much more. In other words, your partner will interact with people you may or may not know in the supermarket, parking lot, work, school, funerals, church, concert, social media, etc. Therefore, each person that your partner interacts with certainly creates a short- or long-term impression on your partner. And the truth is, some of such impressions might have a strong impact on your partner instantly or over time.

Pause for a moment and think about the impression your partner may have after interacting with someone who might be richer, more influential, better-looking, more romantic, more famous, more talented, and more successful than you! Truth be told, irrespective of how long your relationship has been or how close you two are, you can't prevent your partner's mind from receiving an impression as they interact with this person. Therefore, after your partner has interacted with the best of others, what is the guarantee that the impression you create in your partner's mind will be the strongest and oldest?

Also, as the days go by, people and various circumstances will create cracks in your relationship in one way or another. Sadly, these cracks might sooner or later develop into holes. As a result, *cankerworms* will slide in and destroy the romance, joy, heat, trust, faithfulness, and affection between you two. Therefore, you need that factor which will glue the cracks, destroy the existing cankerworms in your relationship, and elevate you above everyone. I have termed the said factor as *the glue factor*.

But what is *the glue factor*? With emphasis, I must say that these days, people are more attracted to those who are rich, famous, successful, and sexually and physically appealing. And it is believed that when you have a partner who has these qualities, you have it all. But do riches, fame, success, sex, and looks really glue a relationship together? And if they do, to what extent? Also, how effective are they in binding relationships?

Well, let me assure you that if you can tell me why a famous guy will break up with a famous lady for an infamous lady, then I will tell you how long fame can be a glue factor. And if you can tell me why a business mogul is dumped for a commoner, then I'll tell you how effective money can glue a relationship together. The point is, though there are many glue factors, there is one that lasts forever. It's the most effective and reliable; this is the one I call *the glue factor* and will elaborate about it in the succeeding paragraphs in this chapter.

So what really is *the glue factor*, and how different is it from other glue factors? Well, after you have talked about what you know, what you have achieved, how special you are, and where you've been, kindly answer these questions: When all is said and done, who are you? If we have to keep what you boast of aside, who are you? For example, do I have to see beauty in you because of your looks? If that is the case, the day an ailment deforms you or when I interact with someone more beautiful and seductive, I won't see anything peculiar about your beauty. Therefore, what do I get when all is said and done? Whom do I find behind the mask? Who are you apart from what people see on the outside? Do you have what it takes to erase all my excuses from cheating on you even though I'll always have the chance to? Do you have what it takes to cause me to always crave for you even though you may not be the most charming person I have seen? What aspect about your life guarantees to glue every crack in our relationship irrespective of how severe the cracks may be?

Therefore, *the glue factor* is the *beautified spirit* in a person. A person with this never goes unnoticed; whenever he or she interacts with people, they just like his or her company. You may not be the richest, most good-looking, most successful, or most famous, but you will always naturally attract and win people's affection. With the glue factor in you, whenever you talk, humanity will listen; when you sing, humanity will dance; when you take a step, humanity will follow. Why? Because the spirit of humanity is naturally inclined to a beautified spirit!

Have you ever heard someone say 'She may not be the best, but there is something different about her'? And the truth is, people won't be able to tell exactly what is different about you because it's an aspect that is not external; it can't be touched, measured, and seen, and no one can put a price on it; this is because it can only be *felt*. As a result, when people interact with you, they feel a strong connection they can't explain. And the more beautiful your spirit being is, the more they want to hang around you and the stronger the bond someone will have with you.

I'm not sure if you know about relationships that are highly criticized because those involved aren't a good match in the views of the public. I have heard people say, 'What is such a beautiful and successful lady doing with that ugly dude?' If only they knew what she likes about him . . .

The point I'm trying to make is that when the glue factor becomes a reality in your life, though your partner might have many opportunities to cheat on you, it won't happen. Why? I told you; those with the glue factor have a deeper and more genuine impact on their partners. And no one can break this bond. That is why I must say that the more beautified your spirit being is, the less you'll struggle to keep your relationship together and vice versa.

But why is it that not everybody has the glue factor in them? Well, the truth is, everybody has a spirit in them. But for this spirit to be beautified, another spirit is responsible. This reminds me of a lady who was famous many years ago because of what she had done; she charmed her husband who was young, rich, and an active ladies' man. But after enjoying a faithful man for years, she ran out of luck sooner than expected. The charm was found by her housemaid, so its effect was nullified instantly. To shorten the long story, not only was her husband set free from this charm, but he rushed back to his old ways.

I share this story with you because while he was under that spell, every mistake she made was unnoticed irrespective of how severe it was. In fact, he loved her unconditionally and was always willing to go an extra mile for her in every regard. But the point I am trying to make is that you can have a similar effect she had on her man if only you would beautify your spirit being.

Despite the fact that some people know of this secret, most have rather chosen to ignore it while a few don't believe it at all. Of course, everyone is entitled to their views. But let me share this other story with you. Folks, there was a woman called Jezebel. I am sure this name rings a bell! She was the most feared, deceitful, manipulative, and seductive woman long ago. No man or woman could resist her. Do you know that she even closed down the greatest institutions, broke up numerous *love* relationships, and controlled the economy of her time? Kings and influential men longed for her because of how strange her aura was.

Indeed, I have news for you; today, Jezebel's aura lives just around the place where your partner lives, shops, works, does fellowships, works out, studies, visits, etc. In addition, nowadays, this aura lives in both men and women of all races and ages. That is why a man can easily *snatch* your woman, a woman can easily *snatch* your man, and someone far younger/older can conveniently *snatch* your partner.

Jezebel's aura is very strong and has never struggled power with any other aura; it takes what it wants when and how it wants it and much more. Also, it has no respect for persons, title (engaged or married), how much you love your partner, how many sacrifices you have made for each other, how long you two have been together, and much more.

Therefore, the question at this time should be, is there any other aura that supersedes Jezebel's? Gladly, there is! And if you truly love your partner and want to stick together regardless of the challenges life throws at your relationship, then using this aura I'm about to introduce you to should not be optional. Therefore, ladies and gentlemen, I humbly bring to you the *ultimate glue factor enhancer* and the *only dissolver* of Jezebel's aura, *the Holy Spirit!*

Please get this straight! You can never have it all to please your partner every day throughout your relationship. You will at times make mistakes, some of which will be strong enough to cause a severe crack in your relationship. This is one of those moments that the Holy Spirit steps in and revitalizes your glue factor, thereby restoring your relationship above any flaw. This spirit also knows the exact problems that *will certainly* attack your relationship as well as how you can prevent or overcome them.

The Holy Spirit knows how to make you the most desired person in your partner's heart, irrespective of how advanced your competitors might be. Remember, the more beautified your glue factor is, the more enduring your relationship will be no matter what time brings. And the only way to have this experience is to let the ultimate glue factor enhancer make you a true piece of excellence. And when this happens, your *love* relationship will forever be that place where heat meets romance and the glue factor.

ABOUT THE AUTHOR

As a life and business coach, mentor, public and motivational Speaker, Peter Bate Eta seeks to provide a reliable shoulder on which others can lean on as he journeys with them.